Who is Jesus?

CAROLYN NYSTROM

Illustrated by
Wayne A. Hanna

MOODY PRESS
CHICAGO

For Randy
because
Jesus loves him

© 1980, by
THE MOODY BIBLE INSTITUTE
OF CHICAGO

ISBN: 0-8024-5993-5

Printed in the United States of America

7 Printing/DB/Year 87 86 85 84

Moody Press, a ministry of the Moody Bible Institute,
is designed for education, evangelization, and
edification. If we may assist you in knowing more about
Christ and the Christian life, please write us without
obligation: Moody Press, c/o MLM, Chicago, Illinois 60610.

I have a special friend. Let me tell you about Him. His name is Jesus.

Genesis 1 and 2; John 1:1-14; Revelation 4:11

Long long ago, before there was a world or a star or even a sky, there was Jesus. Together with God, His Father, and God the Spirit, Jesus made the world. He made all the big trees and tiny flowers, and all the animals—the funny rhinocerous and the

gentle puppy. God made the sky and
everything in it. Then God made people—
a man and a woman. The man and woman
loved each other and together they loved God.
Jesus loved them too. He walked and
talked with them every day.

Genesis 3

But one day the man and woman did something wrong. They did not obey God. That is sin. Because God is holy, He could no longer walk and talk with them. So the man and woman had to leave the beautiful place God had made for them. After that they worked hard digging up stones and briars to plant seeds for food. They were often tired and hungry. They had children, and their children sinned too.

Genesis 3:15

But God still loved them. He promised that one day He would send Someone to take away sin.

Isaiah 53:4-6; Micah 5:2

Thousands of years passed. The world filled with people. They all sinned. But over and over God sent men called prophets to remind the people of that special Someone who would make them once again right with God.

Luke 1:26-38; Matthew 1:18-25

Then Jesus came.

God sent His own Son to earth, not as a

powerful king but as a tiny baby. God gave
Jesus a mother named Mary, but God was His
Father. Jesus grew inside Mary's tummy
just like other babies. He was born
like other babies.

God knew that Jesus would need a daddy
to take care of Him while He was growing up,
so Mary's husband, Joseph, became His
adopted daddy.

I like my family. I'm glad Jesus had a
family too.

Luke 2:1-20

Mary and Joseph had to take a long trip to Bethlehem just before Jesus was born. When they got there, Joseph looked hard for a place to sleep, but the town was crowded with other travelers. There was no room left. Finally they found a cave where cows and donkeys stayed. That night Jesus was born. Mary wrapped her new baby in warm cloths and laid Him in a manger to sleep.

Later that night something wonderful happened in a field not far from Bethlehem.

Shepherds were watching their sheep. Suddenly a brilliant light filled the sky, and angels appeared. They told the shepherds that Jesus, the Savior God had promised long ago, was now born. They even told the shepherds where they could find Him in the nearby town. Then the angels shouted praises to God and disappeared into heaven.

The shepherds hurried to see the new baby. They were Jesus' first visitors.

Luke 2:41-52; Mark 6:3

Jesus grew up like other boys in His town. He studied God's Word, the Old Testament Bible. He visited God's house, the Temple. He obeyed His parents. He learned to build with wood because that was His adopted daddy's job. So Jesus became a carpenter.

I wonder if Jesus liked to work with His daddy. I do.

Matthew 4:1-11; Hebrews 4:15

Because Jesus was like other children, He had feelings just like I do. He felt happy

when He played with pebbles in the warm sun. He felt sad when friends were mean to Him. When He fell down and skinned His knees, they hurt—just like mine.

But Jesus was also different from other boys. He was God. He never sinned. Even when Satan, God's greatest enemy, came to Jesus and tried to talk Him into doing wrong, Jesus said no. He remembered what He had studied in the Bible. That helped Him say no to Satan.

Jesus grew up to be a man, just like I will. Then He looked like other men in His part of the world. There, most men had light brown skin and dark hair. They grew their hair and beards long. They wore long loose robes to protect them from the sun and sandals to make it easier to walk over the sandy soil. Jesus walked hundreds of miles so He may have carried a walking stick to help when He got tired. Probably He wrapped a wet turban around His head to keep Him cool on scorching sunny days.

Mark 3:7-19

For three years, Jesus walked up and down His country. He crossed sandy deserts and climbed rocky hills. He traveled across lakes in a small boat. He visited small towns, big cities, and wild empty places in the country. Everywhere, people followed him.

The people wanted Jesus to teach them. So He taught them what He knew from studying the Bible, but He also taught them more. Jesus was God's Son. He had lived with God, His Father, since before the world began. So Jesus taught the people to know God. He taught them how to pray to God, how to please God. And He taught them how to live together without hurting each other.

Once, more than five thousand people followed Jesus to a lonely place to hear Him teach. The people were tired and hungry from the long walk. Jesus felt sorry for them. Maybe He was tired and hungry too. He asked if anyone had food to share. Only one small boy brought his lunch to Jesus. Jesus prayed, thanking His Father for the food. Then slowly He began to break the

boy's bread and fish into small pieces. And the most amazing thing happened. More and more pieces came from the boy's lunch, but Jesus did not run out of food. Jesus' friends passed out bread and fish to the people. They all ate until they were full, even the little boy. Even then, the food was not gone. Twelve basketfuls were left over.

I wonder how that boy felt when he saw his lunch feeding so many people. I wonder if he knew that Jesus had made the whole world, so it would be no trouble to make his lunch into a little extra food.

Mark 2:1-12; Mark 5:21-43; John 9:1-23

Sometimes sick people crowded around Jesus, and He helped them. Jesus made clay for a man who couldn't see from the time he was a baby. He put it on the man's eyes. When the man washed his eyes, he could see.

Friends carried a man who couldn't move at all to see Jesus. Jesus spoke to him, and the man picked up his mat and walked away.

A woman who had been sick for twelve years touched Jesus' clothing, and Jesus made her well.

A twelve-year-old girl died. Jesus came to her house and brought her back to life.

Mark 10:13-16

Once a group of children came to Jesus. His friends told the children that Jesus was tired and they should go away. But Jesus reached out His arms to them and took them on His lap.

I'm glad Jesus takes time for children because I need a lot of time.

Luke 23:1-49

But not everyone loved Jesus. Bad men were afraid of Him because they did not want to change their lives to please God. They were afraid of the big crowds who followed Jesus. So they made up lies about Jesus and told those lies to the governor. Together they decided that Jesus must die. So soldiers nailed Jesus' hands and feet to a cross. That was the way they killed people who disobeyed important laws.

Matthew 26:53-54; John 10:16-18

But Jesus hadn't done anything wrong. Because He is God, He could have come down from the cross if He had wanted to. But He didn't.

I am sad when I think how Jesus died, but I am thankful too—because He did it for me.

John 3:16; Romans 10:9-10; 2 Corinthians 5:21

You see, every person in the world has done wrong—even me. Sometimes no one sees my sin, like the time I took my sister's bubble gum and hid it in my closet. But God knows. And my sin makes Him sad. It makes me sad too. I thought of other things I had done wrong, and I worried that God would punish me.

Then I remembered, *That's why Jesus died. He took the punishment for my sin.* So I prayed, "Jesus, I'm sorry I did wrong. Thank You for taking my punishment. I want to be Yours from now on."

And God forgave me. I am His child for ever and ever.

(I knew Jesus would want me to give Suzy back her gum—so I did, even before she asked.)

After Jesus died on the cross, Jesus' friends were sad and frightened. Some went back to work, others ran away. But three days later something wonderful happened.

Jesus came back alive!

Luke 24:13-53

For many days He walked and talked with His friends. They could touch Him. Once Jesus even cooked breakfast for them. He taught them to understand the Bible better than they ever had before. Then one day Jesus gathered His friends together. While they were all watching, Jesus was lifted straight up into heaven.

Romans 8:34; Hebrews 7:25

Do you wonder what Jesus does in heaven? He hears and answers prayers—the prayers of all His people on earth (mine too).

John 14:1-7

And He is making heaven ready for us to come and live with Him. I can't imagine what heaven is like, but if Jesus makes it for me, I know I'll like it.

1 Thessalonians 4:13-18

But the best part of Jesus' story hasn't happened yet. Jesus is coming back to earth! All of us who love Jesus will be caught up to meet Him in the air. Even people who have died will come back to life, just as He did.

Revelation 1:8; Revelation 5:11-14

And we shall live with Jesus in heaven for ever and ever.

Jesus is my special friend, but He is much more than a friend; He is my God.

So I pray to Him.

I try to do what is right, because I know Jesus wants me to.

I thank Jesus for dying for me.

Even when I'm sad, I remember, *Jesus loves me.* And I feel warm and snuggly inside.

Jesus loves you too. He wants to be your friend. Why don't you ask Him?